EXPLORING

THE PRACTICE OF ENTREPRENEURSHIP

REBECCA J. WHITE, PHD

Dedication

"The pessimist complains about the wind; the optimist expects it to change; the realist adjusts the sails."

William Arthur Ward

To Captain Giles, with gratitude for our life together
and for adjusting the sails when needed.

Foreword

In Dr. White's new Guidebook, *Exploring the Practice of Entrepreneurship,* she states that every entrepreneur's experience is an experiment. The very practice of entrepreneurship is about making and testing assumptions to reach the desired outcome. Along the way the outcomes will often not match expectations. In essence she describes that the very nature of entrepreneurs must "remain teachable". This quote is resident on my email signature line as I push this ideal out to the world every time I send or reply to an email in business. Remaining coachable, teachable and always being open to new ways to succeed is a fundamental I personally believe can be a part of the secret sauce for successful entrepreneurship.

Dr. White has not only written a book on how to become a successful entrepreneur, she teaches while describing the fundamentals of self-leadership. This Guidebook, directs you through, how to overcome fear, self-doubt and how to be honest with yourself in a way that entrepreneurs need to understand.

The pages of this book are packed with tools on "how to" and "what not to do" while making your way through the behaviors of becoming an entrepreneur, which is backed by research and science base facts. The number of personal stories from her university classroom and her podcast interviews were influential in driving home these facts.

The See, Do, Repeat model is exactly what we do in the maritime industry in training our crews on safety and customer care. And I personally loved the reference about being the captain of your own ship. **As a captain,** I have found that making the final decision is not always easy and comes with great responsibility especially when all odds are against you. Dr. White is correct in stating, sometime it can be lonely.

I'm certain after reading this book, you will believe as I do that it will add value to your life. It has given me some extra tools to use when I embark on another journey across the Mediterranean Sea and it will most assurably help every entrepreneur on their own journey.

To sum up, my takeaway from reading this book is:

To SEE is to DO and once we SEE and DO we must REPEAT in order to learn how to continue to SEE and DO.

Captain Sandy Yawn
Founder & CEO, Captain Sandy Inc.
Bravo TV Star & One of the Most Respected Captains in the Industry

Introduction

ABOUT THIS BOOK AND ASSESSMENT

This Guidebook, *Exploring the Practice of Entrepreneurship*, and its companion assessment will help you build your own entrepreneurial practice. They follow the principles outlined in *See, Do, Repeat: The Practice of Entrepreneurship*.[1] When used together, the assessment, exercises and suggestions in this guidebook will help you build your practice on the three primary competencies of entrepreneurship. These principles come from more than 30 years of studying and practicing entrepreneurship. After countless research studies, hundreds of interviews and conversations with entrepreneurs from across industries and demographics and my personal experience as an entrepreneur, I wanted to share what I learned.

My findings led to some powerful discoveries that, in the end, are quite simple and elegant. First, despite the uniqueness of each entrepreneurial endeavor, there is a common mindset that drives the actions and choices of entrepreneurs. Second, while they all depend upon a common set of abilities and skills to develop these competencies, successful entrepreneurs seek help when they don't possess a necessary skill or ability. Third, the more they develop their mindset, the more likely they attract others who can fill in the gaps.

The research, interviews and experiences began to tell a story of mindset, intention and attraction. From this work, three entrepreneurial competencies emerged. These three competencies then provided a model for creating a learning path for the experience and practice of entrepreneurship that I share with my students and clients and with you in this guidebook.

The ability to recognize entrepreneurial opportunities

The willingness to act on them

The resilience to execute past failure

The See, Do, Repeat (SDR) model is not just a set of competencies and skills required for any entrepreneurial endeavor. They are also the customized, experiential pathway to gain those skills and the entrepreneurial mindset. This guidebook will show you step-by-step how to apply and work toward these competencies.

Remember, the practice of entrepreneurship is like any other practice. I often compare it to the practice of yoga, but you can also think of any skill you want to attain. The most important step is to show up every day and do the work. Some days will be great, others will be... well, there may be days you want to forget and never experience again. However, that is when you can go back to the basics, focus on areas you can control and keep moving forward because that is the real difference between those who succeed and those who don't. Successful entrepreneurs keep showing up. They are willing to continue to move past failure and adversity.

WHY THIS WORKS

The program outlined for you here is based on principles of *self-explored learning*. This kind of learning includes an interplay between two types of experiences.

⇨ *Self-inquiry* is the thoughtful process of discovering yourself through reflection on past experiences and acknowledging patterns in your interests, habits and strengths as they relate to the **See, Do, Repeat** competencies.

⇨ *Self-directed learning* is applying what you discover through self-inquiry, creating a personalized learning approach that accounts for the current situation, applying tools to enact the plan, identifying learning and accountability partners and monitoring progress along the way.

To meet the goals of a learning program based on self-exploration, we designed this program to include assessments and suggested exercises you can put together in the best way for you. Self-explored learning is empowering, deeply personal and customizable to meet the needs of any learner. It can also provide *just in time* learning, that is, learning when needed while remaining *transformational* over the long term. This is the kind of education most entrepreneurs value.

SUGGESTIONS ON HOW TO START YOUR OWN SELF-EXPLORED LEARNING PROGRAM:

This guidebook and the companion assessment can help you start on your entrepreneurial journey. They can also help you stay on track if you have already launched one or more entrepreneurial ventures. In this book, you will find the material presented in three sections based on the SDR model. Each section has several abilities or skills required for the associated competency. Each chapter starts with an overview of how each skill or ability relates to successful entrepreneurial practice. Then, there's a brief overview of the key concepts you must first know and understand before beginning your practice.

Once you understand the basics for each skill, you're ready to dig into the practice. As you use this book, refer to the *See, Do, Repeat: The Practice of Entrepreneurship*.

Each chapter provides you with three levels of practice based on a continuum of learning from awareness to mastery. The first set of exercises includes ways to expand your understanding; this is the *knowledge* level. The second set of exercises (*application*), offers some suggestions on how to experience what you've learned. The third set of exercises provides ways to develop *mastery*. To get the most out the exercises in this book, work on each of these *in order*. Once you've invested time into developing your knowledge, you can then move on to the application and if desired, you may choose to work toward proficiency in one or all of these skills over time.

Many often think entrepreneurship is a lonely experience. Entrepreneurs do often have to step out and take action that others may not understand. Similarly, each individual's practice of entrepreneurship is a deeply personal experience. There are exercises in this program that require you to dig deep and learn more about yourself.

However, entrepreneurship is also a social experience. Like most other endeavors in life, much of the work of an entrepreneur depends on working with and through others. This practice includes both solo and team experiences.

As you work through these exercises, you can learn via collaboration, mentoring/coaching, reflection, apprenticeship and multiple practices. Throughout the process, keep a journal, seek out stories of entrepreneurs via books, podcasts or personal conversations and even form communities of like-minded people.

As the designer of your own entrepreneurial journey and practice, there is no "best" way to use this guidebook. However, this guidebook can provide you with a step-by-step guide that can help you to take your idea to launch. If you are exploring entrepreneurship for the first time or just starting on your entrepreneurial endeavor, work through the chapters *in the order provided*. For some topics, you may want to take a shallow dive and then return to work on proficiency at a later time. Stay on that skill until you have at least taken some steps toward understanding. If you have already launched your own business or are using this guidebook as a refresher course, you may want to skip right to the areas where you believe you have the greatest need right now and then return to others at a later time.

Regardless of how you choose to use this guidebook to build your practice, consider this a journey rather than a quick fix or a life hack. These skills develop over a lifetime. You do not need to become an expert in them all before you launch a new venture. In fact, taking the step to launch or grow your company while you are working on these skills and abilities is likely to enhance your learning. And if you are already running your own company, this guidebook can provide some assistance as you face the inevitable challenges of entrepreneurship.

TAKING THE FIRST STEP

It's a good idea to take the *See, Do, Repeat Competency* Assessment *before* you begin. This test is a useful self-awareness tool designed to help you better understand where you are now and where you might consider investing time and energy to advance your entrepreneurial practice. While reading the book, take this assessment (drrebeccawhite. com/see-do-repeat#assessment/) again to assess your personal growth and development.

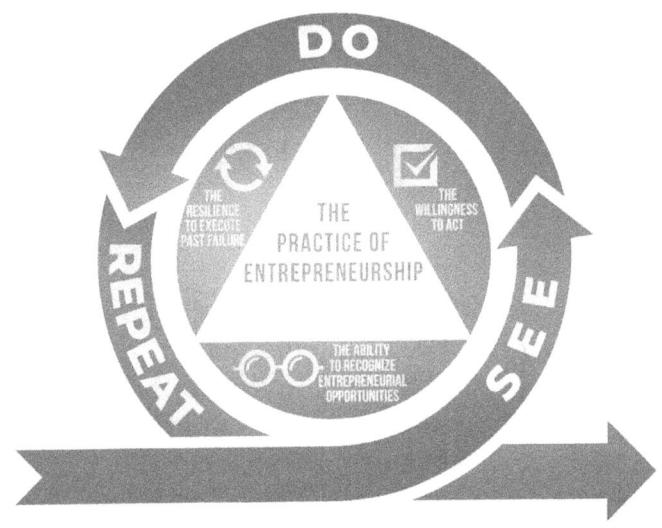

Chapter 1

> **❝** *Opportunities are like sunrises;*
> *if you wait too long, you miss them.*

—William Arthur Ward

MOTIVATION

The practice of entrepreneurship begins with the ability to recognize opportunities. It is one of the key competencies that entrepreneurs depend on for their success. Do you know anyone who always seems to have great ideas or someone for whom opportunities seem to materialize on a regular basis? Perhaps you think there are special people who were born with some unique genetic code for recognizing. Or, like many people, you're afraid you aren't creative, so this competency isn't something you can master? But the ability to consistently see great entrepreneurial opportunities is available to everyone.

It is a process for anyone who wants to do the work necessary to master entrepreneurial opportunities. It's true some people are naturally skilled at some, perhaps many, of the skills in the process. And if you are one of those fortunate people, congratulations. However, for those less fortunate it's still possible to learn the skills to identify entrepreneurial opportunities and even continue to learn and improve.

DEFINITIONS, KEY CRITERIA AND CONCEPTS

Like every skill in the *See, Do, Repeat practice of entrepreneurship*, the ability to recognize opportunities requires three levels of learning: knowledge, application and mastery. Let's start with learning the basics of entrepreneurial opportunity recognition. Below are a few key definitions and concepts you need to know before you begin.

DEFINITIONS

⇨ **Opportunity** – a set of circumstances that makes it possible to do something.

⇨ **Entrepreneurial opportunity** – those situations in which you can introduce new goods, services, raw materials and organizing methods and sell at a cost greater than their production.[2]

ORIGIN

The word opportunity stems from Latin: *ob* (toward) and *portus* (port). The original term: Op-port-tu: refers to the time before ports were dredged, when the captain and crew had to wait for the tide to rise to go into the ports. Sailors use the phrase *ob portus* to denote the best combination of wind, current and tide to sail into port. However, the only way to seize such weather conditions was if the vessel's captain had already sighted the destination port. Knowing the weather conditions without knowing the destination is useless. Therefore, a ship is in a state of *opportunitas* when its captain decides where to go and knows how to get there.

KEY CRITERIA AND CONCEPTS

⇨ Engaging with the world around you is the first step in identifying entrepreneurial opportunities. Opportunities emerge from the space where the entrepreneur and the environment overlap.

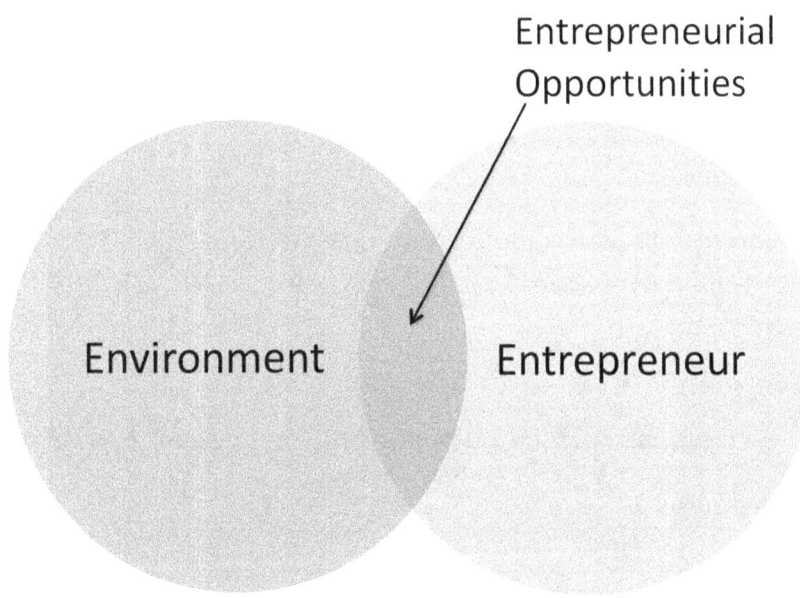

Shane and Venkatraman, 2000

⇨ Ideas are not opportunities. Ideas are necessary but not sufficient. Opportunities begin with a thought, but you must evaluate them to determine whether they are feasible and impactful.

⇨ There are four criteria for an entrepreneurial opportunity:

1   An opportunity is an idea that is ***interesting*** and ***attractive*** for the potential entrepreneur. It is worth pursuing.

2   A viable opportunity must be ***timely***. Like the captain and the crew, an entrepreneur must pay attention to the market's "tides". Launching a concept too soon or too late can be disastrous.

3   An entrepreneurial opportunity has to bring ***rewards*** (usually financial but may also be social) to those who invest time and money into the concept.

4   A viable entrepreneurial opportunity must ***add value*** to the customer.

EXERCISES AND APPLICATION FOR YOUR PRACTICE

Before you begin the exercises in the chapter, complete the following:

LEARNING GOAL(S)

MY MOTIVATION

WHO WILL HELP HOLD ME ACCOUNTABLE?

WHAT ARE MY CURRENT STRENGTHS?

HOW DO I KNOW WHETHER I HAVE REACHED MY GOAL(S)?

ARE THERE OTHER PEOPLE I CAN LEARN WITH OR FROM?

WHAT ARE MY CURRENT CONSTRAINTS?

The ability to recognize opportunities begins with awareness.

To find connections, we first have to disconnect. Taking time to disconnect from our electronics and our busy minds can allow us to *see* differently. How many opportunities are right in front of you but are going unnoticed because you're not paying attention? Consider driving to work, school or the store using a different route this week. Try taking a walk in a different part of your neighborhood or city. What did you notice? Did you see something you didn't see before? Did anything surprise you? Now try talking to someone and listening to them. Ask questions and get to know someone on a deeper level. Find out more about them. Did you learn something new? Maybe you found a new connection.

In the space below, write down at least one new connection you make each day for a week.

MY NEW CONNECTIONS

DAY 1

DAY 2

DAY 3

DAY 4

DAY 5

DAY 6

DAY 7

APPLICATION ASSIGNMENT

PERSONAL COMMITMENT REQUIRED:
20 MINUTES A DAY
AND A CONVERSATION WITH A PEER

Take 20 minutes each day to consider the following and write about it in your opportunity journal. For best results, select a time of the day, e.g., first thing in the morning or during lunch, that will give you the best chance for quiet reflection.

Take a look at the connections you listed in the first section. You don't need to wait until the end of the week. You can start this as soon as you have at least one connection listed. Can you see how that connection can lead to an entrepreneurial opportunity? Push until you can see at least one potential opportunity. It may seem a bit out of reach right now, but that doesn't matter. No one else has to see this.

Now, list as many opportunities as you can see with that connection. Keep trying until you have listed at least five to six ideas for entrepreneurial opportunities. Which one do you think best meets the criteria for an entrepreneurial opportunity? Which one interests you the most and is also timely, has the potential to generate a good return and can bring real value to customers?

Practice this exercise six more times. At the end of seven days of practice, talk to someone you trust about the one you like the most. What do they think about your idea? Don't try to defend your idea right now. Just listen and write down their suggestions on improving your idea to your journal notes for this exercise on page 147. Did you learn something through this collaborative experience?

MASTERY ASSIGNMENT:

PERSONAL COMMITMENT REQUIRED:
20 MINUTES A DAY
& A CONVERSATION WITH
A MENTOR OR COACH

Becoming skilled takes constant practice. For this assignment, make the application exercise a ritual. Carve out 20 minutes each day (at the same time of day) to write about ideas and connections you made during the past 24 hours. Find a mentor or a coach and meet with that person regularly to discuss your ideas. Continue to apply the four criteria to your ideas to see if they are entrepreneurial opportunities before you meet with your coach. A few suggestions about working with a coach:

⇨ **Listen more than you talk**

⇨ **Come prepared each time**

⇨ **Show your gratitude** for the input by thanking them, listening and following up with them on how you used their input. (This doesn't mean you have to take all their advice).

⇨ **Live up to your commitments** – show up on time, follow up with connections and suggestions promptly

⇨ **Remember, it's not all about you**; this is a relationship, and you need to be prepared to give as much as you take

Find a business in the industry that most interests you and seek an internship or apprenticeship with the company. If your current situation doesn't provide room for an internship, create a plan to learn as much as you can about that industry through books, podcasts and talking to people who currently work in that industry.

Chapter 2

> **"** *Opportunity is everywhere.
> The key is to develop the
> vision to see it.*
>
> —Robin Sharma

MOTIVATION

Are you ready to find your next opportunity? If so, it's helpful to know that entrepreneurial opportunities are everywhere. In fact, they're limitless. In the previous chapter, you learned more about the key criteria of an entrepreneurial opportunity. Remember, any idea for a new venture you are considering you must vet to determine whether it is interesting and attractive to you, timely, or provides you with a return that makes it worthwhile and brings value to the customer. In other words, does it have an impact and is it feasible? But before we get to those questions, you have to have an idea first.

You learned in the previous chapter that an idea is necessary but not sufficient as an entrepreneurial opportunity. An entrepreneurial opportunity starts with a thought, an idea. Ideas generate through a creative process you can learn and improve on through practice. Creativity is about connection. It is about engaging with the world and seeking out connections.

Still, it is also about disconnections; getting away from the world, allowing your brain to process the information you absorbed from the world. It requires a yin and yang approach to experience. Too much connection or disconnection can limit the opportunities available to you. Knowing the process and showing up regularly to practice is how creativity works.

But make no mistake, this is hard work. It's not hard because it's complex or complicated. It is hard because it requires discipline and patience. In the end, however, it can become a skill that will set you apart from others. So, let's start on finding your next big opportunity.

KEY CONCEPTS AND THE PROCESS

Each skill in the *See, Do, Repeat practice of entrepreneurship* begins with three levels of learning knowledge, application and mastery. In the previous chapter, you learned the basics of entrepreneurial opportunity recognition. Now, let's turn our attention to understanding the process for developing the vision required to see opportunities everywhere.

KEY CONCEPTS

⇨ **Quantity = Quality** in the generation of creative ideas

⇨ **The ability to recognize opportunities** requires connecting with the world so the diversity of experiences and people available can inspire and influence you

⇨ **Opportunities only become visible when you gain insight and make connections** from what you have learned from connecting with the world, which often requires disconnection from the world

THE PROCESS[3]

Creative problem-solving begins with defining a problem. Once followed, these steps can improve your odds of an outcome in both an innovative and meaningful way. In entrepreneurship, this process can help you recognize more entrepreneurial opportunities.

Collecting raw material: The first step is all about experiences and exposure. The ability to recognize opportunities begins with the collection of information combined to form something new. Remember, opportunities come from ideas generated by combining concepts that already exist only in new and different ways. Exposure to a broad range of experiences will create the quantity of ideas that will lead to higher quality outcomes.

Mental mastication: The mental digestion process occurs when you begin to process the information and data you collected from your experiences. This is where your brain does the work of making connections.

Incubation: This is the disconnection phase of the process. Once you have worked hard to make connections, you must step back and trust the process to work. This may require patience, but you can speed up this process by using techniques like meditation, regularly taking a walk in nature or engaging in other activities that allow your brain to relax and rest.

Illumination: This is the proverbial light bulb stage. You have an idea that seems to have all the required criteria for an entrepreneurial opportunity.

YOUR PRACTICE

Before you begin the exercises in the chapter, complete the following:

LEARNING GOAL(S)

MY MOTIVATION

_____
_____
_____

WHO WILL HELP HOLD ME
ACCOUNTABLE?

_____
_____
_____

WHAT ARE MY CURRENT
STRENGTHS?

_____
_____
_____

HOW DO I KNOW WHETHER I HAVE
REACHED MY GOAL(S)?

_____
_____
_____

ARE THERE OTHER PEOPLE I CAN
LEARN WITH OR FROM?

_____
_____
_____

WHAT ARE MY CURRENT
CONSTRAINTS?

_____
_____
_____

KNOWLEDGE ASSIGNMENT

PERSONAL COMMITMENT REQUIRED:
~3 MINUTES

In the space below, turn each of the circles into a recognizable object.[4]

How did you do? Could you finish all 30?

(Don't feel bad if you didn't, most people do not fill all the circles in three minutes). More importantly, how did you approach this exercise? Were you more focused on getting all 30 designs, or were you more focused on finding unique designs? Or did you try something different? For example, did you lean more toward a derivative approach (e.g., a basketball, soccer ball, a beachball), or did you take a more distinctive approach (e.g., a face, a planet, a pizza)? Did you go outside the assumed rules and combine circles to create eyeglasses or a traffic light? Remember, truly creative solutions are often at the intersection of quantity, diversity, and a willingness to span boundaries.

APPLICATION ASSIGNMENT

PERSONAL COMMITMENT REQUIRED:
30 MINUTES A DAY FOR ONE WEEK

PART 1

Creative problem-solving begins with defining the problem. Problems can be different in many ways, but for this exercise, we will define a problem as a question raised for inquiry, consideration, or solution. In the space below, write down a problem you would like to consider this week. It can be a big, social problem or a more personal problem. It may be a problem you would like to solve through a new venture or by inventing a new product. It doesn't matter which problem you choose for this exercise, but make sure you have sufficient motivation. Be sure it is important enough for you to spend time and effort considering the solution. Once you have chosen the problem, write out the problem and the possible solution in the space below. Then write down two to three reasons why this is a good solution (pros) and two to three reasons why it may not be the best solution (cons).

PROBLEM

SOLUTION

PROS:

_____

_____

_____

CONS:

_____

_____

_____

PART 2

Set aside at least 30 minutes a day to work on this exercise. Complete the steps outlined below for each day.

DAY 1

Read as many pages of newspapers as you can in 30 minutes. If possible, try to read all sections. (The newspaper can be online, but a printed version is better for this exercise.) Think about your problem as you read. Consider if you learn anything in the newspaper that you can connect to your problem. Write down any connections you make. Aim for quantity, diversity and boundary-spanning in your relationships.

DAY 2

Repeat the assignment for Day 1 or read another newspaper. If possible, try finding a newspaper that has a different focus. For example, if you read a national business newspaper the first day, try reading one with a local and more general content the second day.

DAY 3

Review the connections you made on Day 1 and Day 2. Are there any interesting connections or relationships? Pick out the most interesting connection you made and conduct research to learn more about some aspect of that relationship. For example, if you have linked your problem to photography, conduct some research in this field. Find out the trends and the future of photography. Who are the thought leaders in this field? What are they doing, talking about? Keep notes on what you have learned in your journal.

DAY 4

Continue the research you started on Day 3 but focus on a second connection or interesting relationship. Can you also connect this relationship to the one you worked on the previous day? Write down what you have learned in your journal.

DAY 5

Continue to research the topics you identified and keep writing notes about what you have learned.

DAY 6

Today, drop your problem and do something fun during your 30 minutes. Make sure you completely let go of the problem.

DAY 7

Revisit your problem with the information you gathered and fill in the table below. Compare it to what you wrote the previous week. What did you learn? Could you find a better solution? Did the research yield any nuggets of information that can help to solve your problem?

PROBLEM

SOLUTION

PROS:

CONS:

_____

_____

_____

MASTERY ASSIGNMENT

How did the creative problem-solving experiment work for you? How did solution #2 compare to solution #3? During the week, could you generate lots of connections and possible solutions for your problem? Did the process lead to any meaningful insights? If so, that's great. If not, don't worry. The process will work, but it works best when it becomes a habit; the process of creative problem-solving takes time and a certain amount of faith.

To become a powerful idea creator and increase the number of meaningful opportunities in your life, you have to commit time and energy to the process. And you may need to make some changes in your life. Make the process a ritual. Try applying the process to problems daily.

⇨ **Make awareness a habit.** Can you expand your world and knowledge? Maybe you can learn something new, meet some new people, try a new hobby. Expanding your world doesn't require you to spend a lot of money or take an epic trip. It might just mean meeting your neighbors and spending time at the park. There are opportunities all around us. Do you consciously pay attention?

When you travel or experience something new, are you truly exploring the world and people around you, or are you most interested in getting the best photo so you can share it on social media? When you have a conversation with someone, are you listening and learning, or are you spending your time thinking about what you will say? Are there some changes you can make to increase the input of *raw material* in your life?

⇨ **Carve out time each day to write down your ideas and connect them.** Consider getting up 20 minutes earlier every day or taking 20 minutes to write at the end of the day. When you start, don't judge your writing or your connections; just write. The discipline of journaling can be both therapeutic and empowering. Later, spend some time *thinking* about how to connect your ideas to problems to generate creative solutions. Push yourself. When you are really frustrated with the entire process, put it all aside and forget it.

⇨ **Make it a priority to find time regularly to *relax* and forget about the problems you are trying to solve.** Remember this, down time is as important as hard work time.

⇨ **Build in time periodically to reflect on what you have written to see if you have any *insights*.** Did you see anything or someone you met last week who could help you with a problem you are facing today? What kind of connections can you make? What kind of opportunities can you find when you look back?

Chapter 3

“ *I think it's very important to have a feedback loop, where you're constantly thinking about what you've done and how you could be doing it better.*

—Elon Musk

MOTIVATION

In the previous chapter, you had the chance to practice the creative process for generating ideas that may become entrepreneurial opportunities. While the goal of the creative problem-solving process is to get a solution, the "aha" moment is not the final step in this process. In fact, when the proverbial light bulb illuminates, there are quite often many aspects of the solution hidden.

As James Webb Young points out, this stage might be the cold, gray dawn of the morning after. In this stage, you have to take your little idea out into the world of reality.[5] In other words, to ensure the solution is viable and creates value, we must get input. This is the fifth and final stage of the creative problem-solving process and many often refer to it as the *evaluation* stage.

A viable opportunity must first create value for the customer. Creating value for the customer can result in value for you and your investors. Without customers, all we have is an idea. Until we test our idea, all we have is a hypothesis based on our assumptions about what customers want or will or won't do. An idea or hypothesis about an opportunity can only be confirmed through feedback. After putting the first four steps of the creative process to work, you may have identified what you believe is a viable solution. Until you have confirmation from the customer, you cannot be confident that your concept is ready.

DEFINITIONS, KEY CRITERIA AND CONCEPTS

Like every skill in the *See, Do, Repeat practice of entrepreneurship*, learning how to create value requires three levels of learning: knowledge, application and mastery. Let's start with learning the basics of value creation. Below are a few key definitions and concepts that you need to know before you begin.

DEFINITIONS AND KEY CONCEPTS

⇨ Creating value requires an ability to stay ***intellectually honest***, that is,

- ▻ Not lying to yourself

- ▻ Not pretending to know the truth when you don't

- ▻ Not omitting relevant facts purposely

- ▻ Giving credit to sources of information where possible

⇨ Creating value requires a willingness to ***seek out input and receive feedback***

> ▸ The earlier you begin to seek input, the sooner you can find out what works

> ▸ Expect your concept to change significantly from idea to venture, so try not to fall in love too soon

⇨ Entrepreneurial opportunities create value for the customer and all who have invested ***time***, ***talent*** or ***treasure*** in the venture

⇨ Entrepreneurial opportunities create value through ***impact*** and ***feasibility***

> ▸ Entrepreneurial impact – designed to create a significant effect on a defined market

> ▸ Entrepreneurial feasibility – financially and technologically possible and produces desired outcomes for the entrepreneur and those who invested.

CRITERIA OF VALUE CREATION

⇨ Value to the customer

- ▶ Ideas become viable entrepreneurial opportunities only after you confirm you can provide customer value

- ▶ Those who are in the market for your product or service will confirm customer value

- ▶ A market must have all of the following:

  - ▷ **prospective buyers/users**

  - ▷ with a **need** (problem)

  - ▷ who **want** your solution (what you are selling) to that problem

  - ▷ have the **financial ability** to buy/use what you are selling, and

  - ▷ are **willing to spend that money** on what you are selling

⇨ Value to investors of time, talent and treasure

- ▶ Markets must be big enough to be worth the investment of resources

- ▶ Customers must be available and accessible

- ▶ Financial return must meet the goals of people who invested

How

YOUR PRACTICE

Before you begin the exercises in the chapter, complete the following:

> **LEARNING GOAL(S)**

MY MOTIVATION

_____
_____
_____

WHO WILL HELP HOLD ME ACCOUNTABLE?

_____
_____
_____

WHAT ARE MY CURRENT STRENGTHS?

_____
_____
_____

HOW DO I KNOW WHETHER I HAVE REACHED MY GOAL(S)?

_____
_____
_____

ARE THERE OTHER PEOPLE I CAN LEARN WITH OR FROM?

_____
_____
_____

WHAT ARE MY CURRENT CONSTRAINTS?

_____
_____
_____

KNOWLEDGE ASSIGNMENT

PERSONAL COMMITMENT REQUIRED:
20 MINUTES

Ideas are not opportunities. A quantity of ideas is necessary for generating viable opportunities, but it is not sufficient. Remember, there are four criteria for viable opportunities: interesting and worthwhile, timely, financially viable and capable of creating value. Thus far, your practice has likely provided you with the information to help you clarify whether the concept is interesting to you and worth pursuing, and the time is right. However, you are probably still unsure about the last two questions. Will any of the ideas I generated be financially worthwhile, and do they create real value? It is time to put your ideas to the test.

Identify an idea or solution to a problem you believe may be an entrepreneurial opportunity. You may choose to consider the problem/solution you worked on in chapter 2, or it may be something entirely different. If you choose something different, unless you have spent considerable time researching the concept, go back and apply the creative problem-solving exercise in the previous chapter to the concept before you move on with this exercise.

Once you are ready, write brief answers to the following questions in the space below. Just answer them right now to the best of your ability. You won't know all the answers right now but make a good guess based on your current understanding of the situation.

WHY DO I WANT TO DO THIS?

WHY IS NOW THE RIGHT TIME?

WHO ARE THE CUSTOMERS?

WHAT IS THE PROBLEM I AM SOLVING FOR MY CUSTOMERS?

DO THESE CUSTOMERS MEET ALL FIVE CRITERIA FOR A VIABLE MARKET? WHY OR WHY NOT?

APPLICATION ASSIGNMENT

PERSONAL COMMITMENT REQUIRED:
AT LEAST 3-4 HOURS

PART 1

It is now time to test our concept. Consider the answers you provided in the knowledge exercise above. Where were you confident in your answers? Where do you need to do some more research? Are you intellectually honest as you consider this entrepreneurial opportunity? Spend time this week searching out even more information about the idea.

PART 2A

Use the XYZ Company example. This exercise aims to force you to get the most relevant information into a very brief and concise executive summary. This can be challenging because you want to include the most relevant data and information on why you believe this is a viable opportunity without getting too far into the weeds on the details.

PART 2B

Make a list of assumptions regarding the viability and feasibility of this business idea. Write these in your journal. Use the list of questions below to think of all the assumptions you have made.

⇨ What assumptions am I making about my interest and ability to produce and sell this product or service?

⇨ What assumptions am I making about the marketplace and the timing for this product or service?

⇨ What assumptions am I making about value creation? For me? For others who will need to invest time and money?

⇨ What assumptions am I making about my ability to provide value to my customers?

PART 3

If you don't have a coach or mentor yet, now is the time to find one. Ideally, you can find someone who has experience or expertise with your product category, industry, or someone who is an entrepreneur. Meet with your coach or mentor to discuss your concept. Send them the one-page overview before the meeting. Listen and consider the input and make changes to your concept where needed. Remember, you may not want to make all the changes recommended.

XYZ, LLC.

One Line Pitch: XYZ promotes organic natural food with a fleet of mobile, technology-based, food trucks called *Natural Foods*.

Business Summary: XYZ's mission is to promote healthy foods while supporting local farmers. We also help students learn about entrepreneurship.

Products & Services: Our unique distribution and staffing model allows customers to purchase natural, local foods near or on university and college campuses. The business model capitalizes on a growing market of young people who wish to improve their health through their food choices. We also plan to use technology to offer self service for many of the items sold.

Unique Business Model: To gain market visibility and impact and to fulfill our goal of supporting the education of college entrepreneurs, we will partner with Collegiate Entrepreneurs Organization (c-e-o.org) chapters on college and universities campuses in the US now and globally in the future. In exchange for a small percentage of the profits, students will assist with the operation of the business.

Market: In 2020, the food truck industry surpassed 1.2 billion dollars. Furthermore, this industry is expected to grow by nearly 5% over the coming year. Our concept also takes advantage of the rapidly growing small farmers market and increasing growth and interest in entrepreneurship education.

Customers: Our customer is young and educated and represents a major growth market for healthy, food on the go.

Go-to-Market Strategy: To validate the product and business model, we will open our first truck in a US mid-western city that is home to a large state university and a small private college. Each of the campuses have a CEO chapter with students who can work for the company to source, prepare and sell food.

Key Strategic Goal 2021: To be first in market with this unique business model.
Key Financial Goal 2021: To reach $900,000 in revenues.

XYZ COMPANY EXAMPLE

Company Logo

Company Profile
URL: N/A
Industry: Food Trucks
Employees: 4
Founded: April 8, 2021

Contact
John Doe
jdoe@xyzcompany.xxx
555-555-5555

Location
101 Main Street
Small Town USA

Financial Information
Company Stage:
Development
Previous Capital: N/A
Monthly Net Burn: N/A
Pre-Money Valuation:
N/A
Capital Seeking:
$350,000

Management
John Doe
Susie Smith
Leslie Jackson

Advisors
Joe Warren, Marketing
Tom McHugh, Financial
Ron Hafner, Distribution
Joe Johnson, Legal

Financials	2021	2022	2023	2024	2025
Revenues	$972,160	$1,944,320	$2,916,480	$3,888,640	$4,860,800
Expenditures	$250,000	$375,000	$475,000	$575,000	$675,000
Net	$752,160	$1,569,320	$2,441,480	$3,313,640	$4,185,800

APPLICATION ASSIGNMENT:

PERSONAL COMMITMENT REQUIRED:
20+ HOURS (PLUS COMPLETIOIN OF THE
EXERCISES IN THE PREVIOUS SECTION)

Now that you have gathered information from your own research and a coach or mentor, it is time to put your concept to the test.

PART 1

Create a Minimum Viable Product (MVP). Before you begin to talk to prospective customers, you should have a working prototype, your first iteration of your product or service, and what we call a minimum viable product. This will take time and effort, but it is worth the effort. In this process, you will learn a lot about your opportunity's viability.

An MVP can be anything from a very basic product you create in your garage or kitchen to working with an engineer and manufacturing firm. It may be a simple landing page or website that you create with a packaged software product. The more you can show the prospective customer what you offer, the better feedback you get from them. Plus, you get the added benefit of what you learn from this process.

PART 2

Take your MVP and interview at least eight to ten people (even more if possible) who fit your profile of an ideal customer. Prepare a list of questions before you meet with them, and make sure you take notes. Get their feedback on your concept. You can create your own questionnaire, or you can use the one included as a guide at the end of this chapter labeled "Sample Questions."

During your interviews, find out as much as you can about how they will use your product. How often would they buy your product or service? What would they be willing to pay for your product or service? Then, consider how their feedback impacts your opportunity. Do you need to make changes? If possible, talk to more people who you believe might fit your ideal customer profile.

PART 3

Refine your one-page overview based on what you have learned from the interviews. Set up another meeting with your coach or mentor and talk about what you learned. Follow up with any advice or suggestions they provide.

PART 4

Repeat all steps, as necessary. Do you need to change your MVP? Do you need a second round of interviews with prospective customers to share what you learned? Do you need to consider different customers? Keep notes of what you are learning in your journal.

EXTRA CREDIT

If you don't have experience in the industry you are considering, see if you can find an opportunity to get an internship or spend time working in a related business. If your current situation doesn't provide room for an internship or another job, create a plan to learn as much as you can about that industry from books, podcasts and by talking to people who are currently working in that industry. If you want to be an expert in your field, get as much experience and insight as possible.

SAMPLE QUESTIONS FOR YOUR CUSTOMER INTERVIEWS:

1   What do you think of this product or service? Why?

2   What are the top two to three ways we can improve this product or service?

3   How do you think you could best use this product or service?

4   What does this product help you do better, or how could this product improve your business (or your life)?

5   What main problem does this product or service solve for you?

6   What other products or services do you use now, or would you consider solving this problem?

7   Are there other benefits of this product or ways to use this product in addition to the product's main purpose or value?

8   What would you be willing to pay for this product or service?

9   How often would you purchase this product or service?

10   What else would you like to tell about your experience or thoughts on this product or service?

Chapter 4

"If I have the belief I can do it, I shall surely acquire the capacity to do it, even if I may not have it at the beginning.

—Mahatma Gandhi

MOTIVATION

Recognizing viable opportunities is a necessity for entrepreneurship, but it is not sufficient. The next step of the *SDR* model is where the practice of entrepreneurship begins to require increased investments of time and money. This is the stage where we become committed and step into the big unknown.

The decision to pursue your entrepreneurial dreams with full force will probably be the time when you begin to make great sacrifices for your vision. You may leave your current job, spend some of your savings and/or decide to forego spending time with friends or family to realize your vision. This is the proverbial fork in the road where some stop and others keep going. Are you ready?

The willingness to start a new business begins with an intention. Moving from intention to action requires believing you can do what it takes to reach your entrepreneurial vision. Psychologists often refer to the belief that we have the capacity to reach our goals as *self-efficacy*. Higher self-efficacy means we can cope better with failure and challenges. Having this kind of confidence in our abilities does not only lead to the first steps into starting a business but will also carry you through the challenges, failures and setbacks that are inevitably on the pathway to success.

Confidence in our entrepreneurial capacities helps reduce the fears associated with risk and the ambiguity of entrepreneurship. Regardless of where you are on your own entrepreneurial journey, taking time to develop a better awareness of your own state of self-efficacy is important to your ability to succeed as an entrepreneur.

DEFINITIONS, KEY CRITERIA AND CONCEPTS

Like every skill in the *See, Do, Repeat practice of entrepreneurship*, the ability to recognize opportunities requires three levels of learning: knowledge, application and mastery. Let's start with learning the basics of building entrepreneurial self-efficacy. Below are a few key definitions and concepts you need to know before you begin.

DEFINITIONS

⇨ **Confidence** – the feeling or belief that you can rely on someone or something

⇨ **Self-efficacy** – a belief in your capacity to reach your goals

⇨ **Entrepreneurial self-efficacy** – confidence in yourself and your entrepreneurial capacities to reach your vision of entrepreneurship

KEY CRITERIA AND CONCEPTS

⇨ Confidence comes from experience

⇨ To build confidence in your entrepreneurial capacities, you have to act

⇨ Four ways you can build self-efficacy

1   Seeking out experiences that allow you to develop your entrepreneurial skills

2   Gaining inspiration and learning by observing and listening to role models

3   Spending time working with coaches and mentors

4   Maintaining a positive outlook on the future

EXERCISES AND APPLICATION FOR YOUR PRACTICE

Before you begin the exercises in the chapter, complete the following:

LEARNING GOAL(S)

MY MOTIVATION	WHO WILL HELP HOLD ME ACCOUNTABLE?	WHAT ARE MY CURRENT STRENGTHS?

HOW DO I KNOW WHETHER I HAVE REACHED MY GOAL(S)?	ARE THERE OTHER PEOPLE I CAN LEARN WITH OR FROM?	WHAT ARE MY CURRENT CONSTRAINTS?

KNOWLEDGE ASSIGNMENT

PERSONAL COMMITMENT REQUIRED:
1-2 HOURS

We always learn something from taking an action; sometimes we learn what to do, sometimes we learn what not to do. Entrepreneurship is always an experiment because we try to influence the future with our actions today; we are never completely certain of outcomes. Like all learning, we come to know the cause and effect over time, and we can make informed decisions about our actions. This is the essence of building your self-efficacy; building confidence in your ability to generate positive outcomes. Think about your confidence in yourself and your ability to do what it takes to be a successful entrepreneur.

PART 1

On a scale of 1-10, how confident are you in your ability to do the following:

_____ complete difficult tasks

_____ design something novel and new

_____ solve unstructured problems

_____ clearly describe problems

_____ ask probing questions to clarify facts

_____ start a new venture

_____ understand and manage finances

_____ convince others to support your vision

_____ communicate with others

_____ remain resilient in the face of failure

_____ **Total Score – out of 100**

PART 2

Ask your coach or mentor or someone you trust to rate you on these items. Have a discussion with them about the differences between your answers and theirs about you. What did you learn? Write about this in your journal. This is hard work, and it is deeply personal. You will make much better progress if you stay open, kind to yourself and non-judgmental.

APPLICATION ASSIGNMENT

PERSONAL COMMITMENT REQUIRED:
45 MINUTES A DAY FOR ONE WEEK
PLUS ONE HOUR

If you scored a perfect 100 on the previous experiment, you are an exception. If you scored less than 100, you are the norm. If your score was low, don't worry. There are many ways to improve your score. Regardless of your score, the most important first step in building entrepreneurial self-assuredness is self-awareness. There are many ways to begin to build entrepreneurial self-efficacy. One of the best ways is to listen to the stories of other successful entrepreneurs. Storytelling gives us a chance to learn through the experiences of others.

 Review what you wrote about in your journal in the previous exercise. In what areas do you lack self-confidence? Where are the gaps in your self-confidence? Do you have the ability to communicate? Are you concerned about your leadership skills or your business knowledge?

 Find one to two podcasts that include stories of entrepreneurs.[6]
Hint: listen to the Enfactor Podcast

 Subscribe to those podcasts and find time each day to listen to at least one story. Look for ways to learn more about your specific areas of concern.

 After one week of listening to these stories, interview an entrepreneur yourself. During this interview, you can focus on gaps you identified in your self-efficacy analysis.

MASTERY ASSIGNMENT

PERSONAL COMMITMENT REQUIRED:
2-5+ HOURS

There are many ways to build entrepreneurial self-assuredness. Taking classes, working with a mentor or coach, and staying positive about the future are all ways to enhance your self-efficacy. One way to jump-start building this process is to prepare and give an *entrepreneurial pitch*.

An entrepreneurial pitch verbally communicates your business concept in a brief and concise manner. You can also create and prepare slides to support your message. Use the information below to prepare a two- to five-minute pitch and slide deck. Practice your pitch until you are confident in your message. Ask your mentor to listen to your pitch and review your slides and provide feedback. Once you feel comfortable with your pitch, consider taking it to a competition or share it with people who can help you with your business concept.

PART 1

Write 1-2 sentences to answer each of the following:

INTRODUCE YOURSELF AND YOUR VENTURE

TELL A BRIEF STORY OR PROVIDE SOME INFORMATION THAT CATCHES THE LISTENER'S ATTENTION AND GIVES YOU CREDIBILITY

EXPLAIN WHO YOUR CUSTOMER IS

DESCRIBE (VERY BRIEFLY) YOUR CUSTOMER'S PROBLEM

DESCRIBE THE SOLUTION TO THEIR PROBLEM (IN TERMS OF CUSTOMER BENEFITS)

EXPLAIN HOW YOU WILL MAKE MONEY

BRIEFLY LIST YOUR KEY COMPETITORS

EXPLAIN WHY YOUR VENTURE IS BETTER

ASK FOR HELP WITH SOMETHING (AT THIS POINT, IT WILL PROBABLY BE FOR ADVICE, INTRODUCTIONS, THE MONEY ASK MAY COME LATER.)

PART 2

Take what you wrote and prepare no more than five to six slides to support your message. If you haven't yet prepared presentation slides, do some research on how to prepare a good slide deck.

EXTRA CREDIT

Take your pitch and enter a competition where you may win money or other valuable resources.

Chapter 5

> **"** *The true method of knowledge is experiment.*
>
> —William Blake

MOTIVATION

Every new venture is an opportunity to learn because it is an experiment. Entrepreneurship begins with a belief that is based on a lot of assumptions. We have to test all these assumptions because we cannot predict what will happen in the future.

Remember that entrepreneurship resides at the intersection of the entrepreneur and the environment. We change, and our environment changes. Throughout the process, the entrepreneur is learning and adjusting – testing assumptions and making changes, as needed. Learning is at the very core of the entrepreneurial process and the practice of entrepreneurship. As an entrepreneur, you are always learning about yourself, your concept and your environment. The more you learn, the better prepared you are to make good decisions for yourself and your venture.

Successful entrepreneurs are good learners, and they are constantly seeking to learn what they need to know to optimize decision-making. They are willing to invest in formal education when needed. They are skilled at self-directed education and are willing to seek out help with this process, when needed.

DEFINITIONS, KEY CRITERIA AND CONCEPTS

Like every skill in the *See, Do, Repeat practice of entrepreneurship*, the ability to recognize opportunities requires three levels of learning: knowledge, application and mastery. Let's start with learning the basics of designing an entrepreneurial education. Below are a few key definitions and concepts you need to know before you begin.

DEFINITIONS

⇨ **Formal education** – structured learning, which often includes classroom instruction, web-based training, e-learning courses, seminars, webinars, etc. In formal learning, the instructor determines what the student needs to learn.

⇨ **Informal education** – learning that occurs through conversation, and the exploration and enlargement of experience. Sometimes, there is a clear objective link to some broader plan, but not always.

⇨ **Self-directed education** – taking the initiative, with or without the help of others, in deciding on what to learn and how to learn. This includes setting learning goals, finding resources for learning, implementing strategies to learn and assessing learning.

KEY CONCEPTS AND CRITERIA

⇨ Most entrepreneurs rely on a combination of formal and informal learning

⇨ Entrepreneurs become proficient at self-directed education

⇨ A self-directed education for entrepreneurs is intentional, diverse and continuous

⇨ Entrepreneurship is at the intersection of disciplines and typically requires a combination of learning about a specific industry, field or domain (e.g., health care, technology, or music) and business

⇨ Formal educational opportunities to gain skills may be available in formal degree programs, courses and community-sponsored classes or seminars

⇨ Informal education is as important for entrepreneurs as formal education

⇨ To enhance informal educational opportunities, consider these options:

  ▸ Collaborating with others to explore and learn together

  ▸ Learning through coaches or mentors

  ▸ Use a journaling practice to reflect and deepen learning

  ▸ Seek out apprenticeship and internship

  ▸ Making intentional learning a habit

EXERCISES AND APPLICATION FOR YOUR PRACTICE

Before you begin the exercises in the chapter, complete the following:

WHAT ARE MY LEARNING GOAL(S)

MY MOTIVATION

_____

_____

_____

WHO WILL HELP HOLD ME ACCOUNTABLE?

_____

_____

_____

WHAT ARE MY CURRENT STRENGTHS?

_____

_____

_____

HOW DO I KNOW WHETHER I HAVE REACHED MY GOAL(S)?

_____

_____

_____

ARE THERE OTHER PEOPLE I CAN LEARN WITH OR FROM?

_____

_____

_____

WHAT ARE MY CURRENT CONSTRAINTS?

_____

_____

_____

KNOWLEDGE ASSIGNMENT

PERSONAL COMMITMENT REQUIRED:
30-45 MINUTES

The practice of entrepreneurship is about learning. Spend time journaling about your experience with learning. Use the following questions to frame your reflection.

What kind of learner are you?

Are you often anxious or nervous in formal learning experiences?

Do you frequently seek out learning experiences on your own?

How does it feel to be a beginner?

Do you learn best when someone demonstrates what you need to learn?

Do you learn best when you listen and write out what you are hearing?

Do you learn best by taking direction from others?

Do you learn best by trial and effort and by doing it yourself to see what happens?

Do you prefer to learn alone, or are you someone who learns better in a more social setting?

Are you a quick learner, or do you need time to process?

What learning experiences have been the most fun for you?

Which learning experiences have been the most challenging?

APPLICATION ASSIGNMENT

PART 1

Conduct a skills gap analysis.

⇨ Review the list of basic business skills in Chapter 5 of the SDR book. Which topics are you comfortable with and which ones make you pause? Make a list of the subject areas where you believe some additional education could be helpful.

⇨ Take the EMP[7] and the **See, Do, Repeat** competency assessment[8] and learn more about yourself and your own mindset. Are there mindset skills you would like to enhance or develop?

PART 2

Create a self-directed and dynamic learning plan. Meet with your coach and enlist their help with starting your own self-directed learning plan. Decide on two areas from the gaps analysis (with the help of your coach) that are most important to you. Write out your plan for these two goals below. Begin by listing each learning goal.

You may want to learn the basics of social media marketing. Then, list the format for this learning that you and your coach believe is most appropriate for you based on your learning style and the topic. For example, you may want to take an online seminar. You should consider who can help you with this goal. Because you are new to this topic, you may want to enlist someone who is an expert or is familiar with social media marketing. Or, if you learn better with a peer, you may want to invite someone to be part of a learning group to collaborate with you while learning.

After completing the online seminar, you can write the date completed and write any notes for follow-up. For example, after the webinar, if you want to learn more, you may take an advanced program. Or perhaps if you want to practice what you have learned, you can set a goal to apply what you've learned.

	AREA 1	AREA 2
LEARNING GOAL		
LEARNING FORMAT		
WHO CAN HELP		
DATE COMPLETED		
FOLLOW-UP		

MASTERY ASSIGNMENT:

PERSONAL COMMITMENT REQUIRED:
A LIFETIME

Use the process in the previous example to develop your own entrepreneurial education plan. Learning is naturally a part of the practice of entrepreneurship. You will learn with every step and action you take toward reaching your entrepreneurial goals. However, mastery of an entrepreneurial education comes when you are intentional with your learning.

You may decide that you learn best in a formal setting and if so, you may choose to enroll in a degree program that will provide the goals, format, guidance and a definite completion date. On the other hand, you may decide that you want a more informal education, or you may want to use a combination of the two. Regardless, you can use the exercise in the preceding section to write out your own plan for entrepreneurial education. Remember that you will need to constantly revisit and revise the plan since entrepreneurship is a learning journey each day.

As you build your own educational plan, remember to consider the different ways you can learn. If you are a social learner, consider creating a mastermind group of others who want to learn about similar topics. Together, you can collaborate on your learning and hold each other accountable. If you learn better with direction, you may want to seek a coach or mentor to guide your learning and help you reach your goals.

If you are more of a solitary learner, you can find lots of content online and in books. If you learn better by doing, try to find an opportunity to work in an internship or take a job in an industry of interest. Figure out what works best and prioritize learning in your entrepreneurial practice.

List of Important Business Skills

 Accounting: the language of business. Basics you need to know

- ▸ Terminology

- ▸ Margin

- ▸ Cash flow

- ▸ Understanding the financial levers that drive your business

- ▸ How to read basic financial statements

- ▸ Funding your venture

- ▸ How to find the right accountant

 Risk mitigation and regulation: knowing how to protect yourself and your assets

- ▸ Legal entity formation

- ▸ Intellectual property protection

- ▸ Contracts

- ▸ Insurance

- ▸ Licensing and permits

- ▸ How to find the right attorney

Business models and strategy: how to plan and share that plan

- ▶ Key components of a business plan

- ▶ Business model canvas

- ▶ How to conduct business research

- ▶ How to build an operational plan

- ▶ How to communicate and pitch your vision and strategy

 Marketing: knowing how to identify and communicate with your audience

- ▶ Defining a market

- ▶ Accessing a market

- ▶ Reaching a market

- ▶ Messaging

- ▶ Metrics

 People: knowing how to build a team

- ▶ Load the bus first philosophy

- ▶ Understanding key components of a team

- ▶ Creating a shared vision[9]

- ▶ Understanding how to manage and lead

Chapter 6

> " *Your network is your net worth.*
>
> —Porter Gale

MOTIVATION

It is no secret that networking is important to entrepreneurs. Launching a new venture involves bringing together the resources – the people, money, and strategic assets – that an opportunity requires. Entrepreneurs decide to pursue viable opportunities regardless of whether they initially have access to the resources they need. In fact, in most cases, they challenge entrepreneurial opportunities despite *not* having the resources they need. Connecting with the right people can make the difference in whether or not you can get the resources you need.

For every entrepreneur, their network is one of their most valuable assets. Your network is your social capital. Just like money, building your network is one of the most important skills you can develop in the practice of entrepreneurship. It is also one of the most challenging to get right. Building a network can take a lot of time and effort. While many events and programs can provide a venue for meeting and interacting with people who could be helpful to your cause, not all of these are equal.

And, while showing up and following up are two requirements of impactful networking, these alone are not sufficient. Figuring out who you need to foster relationships with, how to connect with them and ensure those relationships pay off for your business is key to building your entrepreneurial network. And with this skill, mastery comes by knowing how to manage and maintain the relationships in your network.

DEFINITIONS, KEY CRITERIA AND CONCEPTS

Like every skill in the *See, Do, Repeat practice of entrepreneurship*, the ability to recognize opportunities requires three levels of learning: knowledge, application and mastery. Let's start with learning the basics of networking and building your social capital. Below are a few key definitions and concepts you need to know before you begin.

DEFINITIONS

⇨ **Networking** – the process entrepreneurs use to gain social capital

⇨ **Social capital** – provides the relationships through which an entrepreneur receives access to human, financial and other strategic assets

⇨ **Networks of social capital** include both strong ties and weak ties

  ▸ **Strong ties** (family members and close friends) are important to provide support and friendship to an entrepreneur.

  ▸ **Weak ties** (acquaintances and distant social relationships) are important for building entrepreneurial social capital

⇨ **Entrepreneurial ecosystems** are networks of individuals engaged in entrepreneurship or support entrepreneurship with a common goal of advancing entrepreneurial outcomes

KEY CRITERIA AND CONCEPTS

⇨ A broad and diverse network is more beneficial for entrepreneurs because it can bring increased access.

⇨ Engaging with entrepreneurial ecosystems can jump-start your social capital.

⇨ Networks are people and are dependent upon relationships.

⇨ Healthy relationships are reciprocal, and it is important to give as well as take (i.e., it is not just about you).

⇨ Networks need managing and will change over time as your situation changes.

⇨ Strategic networking steps

  ▸ Understand why you are building your network

  ▸ Research opportunities to connect

  ▸ Learn something about other people who may attend this event

  ▸ Create and refine your pitch

  ▸ Become an expert at asking questions that lead to meaningful conversation

  ▸ Listen more than you talk

  ▸ Networks are relationships – give as much or more than you take

  ▸ Protect people in your network by requesting permission before you connect them with others

EXERCISES AND APPLICATION FOR YOUR PRACTICE

Before you begin the exercises in the chapter, complete the following:

WHAT ARE MY LEARNING GOAL(S)

MY MOTIVATION

WHO WILL HELP HOLD ME ACCOUNTABLE?

WHAT ARE MY CURRENT STRENGTHS?

_____

_____

_____

HOW DO I KNOW WHETHER I HAVE REACHED MY GOAL(S)?

ARE THERE OTHER PEOPLE I CAN LEARN WITH OR FROM?

WHAT ARE MY CURRENT CONSTRAINTS?

_____

_____

_____

KNOWLEDGE ASSIGNMENT

PERSONAL COMMITMENT REQUIRED:
~1 HOUR

Entrepreneurs don't let a lack of resources hinder them. The ability to secure resources is a defining attribute of the practice of entrepreneurship. The network of individuals you know is one of the most important assets you have as an entrepreneur. Your social capital is even more important in many ways than financial capital because your network is often instrumental in helping you get the resources you need.

PART 1

Use the questions below to take inventory of your social capital.

Are you flush with connections, or is your social capital account low?

With respect to your entrepreneurial goals, do you have the social capital you need already?

Do you have close ties with whom you can share the emotional and personal side of your entrepreneurial practice?

Do you have a large, diverse network of people who can help you gain access to everything else you need – people, capital and access?

How comfortable are you with networking?

Does the mere thought of a networking event exhaust you?

Do you love to meet new people?

PART 2

Create a networking matrix. When you first start, it can be very helpful to think about how your network can help you access what you need. Using the tables on the next few pages, identify your key resource needs. The most common are in the list already (e.g., connections to money or industry experts, prospective partners, key employees, assets, skills, money), but there is room for you to add others specific to your needs. For now, just think about what you need the most. You will work with your coach/mentor to fill in the rest of the table.

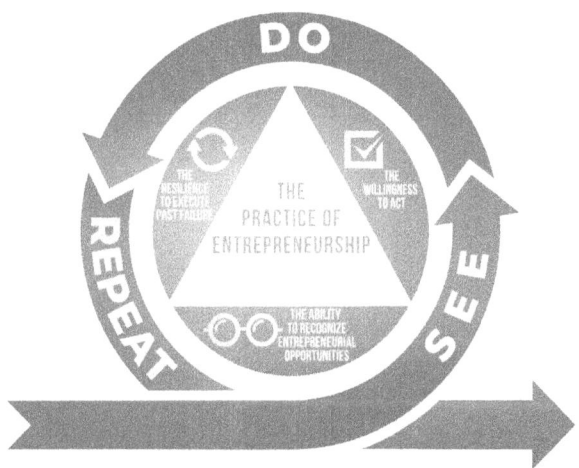

NAME AND CONTACT INFORMATION:

CONNECTIONS: **KEY ASSETS:**

EXPERTISE OR SKILLS: **MONEY:**

POTENTIAL PARTNERS: **PROSPECTIVE EMPLOYEES:**

NAME AND CONTACT INFORMATION:

CONNECTIONS: **KEY ASSETS:**

EXPERTISE OR SKILLS: **MONEY:**

POTENTIAL PARTNERS: **PROSPECTIVE EMPLOYEES:**

NAME AND CONTACT INFORMATION:

CONNECTIONS: KEY ASSETS:

EXPERTISE OR SKILLS: MONEY:

POTENTIAL PARTNERS: PROSPECTIVE EMPLOYEES:

NAME AND CONTACT INFORMATION:

CONNECTIONS: KEY ASSETS:

EXPERTISE OR SKILLS: MONEY:

POTENTIAL PARTNERS: PROSPECTIVE EMPLOYEES:

NAME AND CONTACT INFORMATION:

CONNECTIONS: **KEY ASSETS:**

EXPERTISE OR SKILLS: **MONEY:**

POTENTIAL PARTNERS: **PROSPECTIVE EMPLOYEES:**

NAME AND CONTACT INFORMATION:

CONNECTIONS: **KEY ASSETS:**

EXPERTISE OR SKILLS: **MONEY:**

POTENTIAL PARTNERS: **PROSPECTIVE EMPLOYEES:**

NAME AND CONTACT INFORMATION:

CONNECTIONS: **KEY ASSETS:**

EXPERTISE OR SKILLS: **MONEY:**

POTENTIAL PARTNERS: **PROSPECTIVE EMPLOYEES:**

NAME AND CONTACT INFORMATION:

CONNECTIONS: **KEY ASSETS:**

EXPERTISE OR SKILLS: **MONEY:**

POTENTIAL PARTNERS: **PROSPECTIVE EMPLOYEES:**

NAME AND CONTACT INFORMATION:

CONNECTIONS: **KEY ASSETS:**

EXPERTISE OR SKILLS: **MONEY:**

POTENTIAL PARTNERS: **PROSPECTIVE EMPLOYEES:**

NAME AND CONTACT INFORMATION:

CONNECTIONS: **KEY ASSETS:**

EXPERTISE OR SKILLS: **MONEY:**

POTENTIAL PARTNERS: **PROSPECTIVE EMPLOYEES:**

APPLICATION ASSIGNMENT

PERSONAL COMMITMENT REQUIRED:
3-5+ HOURS

PART 2

Create and refine your pitch. Before you act on the information, you begin to build the social capital you want to make sure you have an elevator pitch. This is a short (90 seconds or less) pitch that you can use to tell someone you meet about your business concept. The name comes from the idea that you should tell your story to someone in the amount of time it would take you to ride up or down an elevator with someone.

Your pitch should be brief and persuasive while also comfortable and authentic. Use the same outline you used in creating your pitch in the Mastery Assignment in Chapter 4 to build your pitch. Make sure you think about requests you can make, depending on your audience. Practice your pitch until you are comfortable, and it feels natural. Make sure you also time yourself and keep your pitch less than 90 seconds.

PART 2

Practice your elevator pitch with your coach and people you trust, and whose opinions you value. Make sure you practice with a few people who know nothing about your concept and see if you can explain your concept clearly and concisely.

PART 3

Share your networking matrix with your coach and see if they have any suggestions for people you should include.

EXTRA CREDIT

See if your entrepreneurial ecosystem has any pitch competitions you can enter, take your new pitch there, and get some practice!

MASTERY ASSIGNMENT

PART 1

Create and convene a peer group focused on working together to build social capital. Identify two to four others who are around the same stage of entrepreneurship as you. If you are just starting, start building your social capital with them. If you already launched your company but are in the early stages of growth and development, try to find a few others who are also at this stage. If you are a more seasoned entrepreneur, look for others who might want to devote time to building social capital together. You can call on your coach to help you find people who might participate.

PART 2

Work with your peer group to build a social capital plan for each member. Ideas for how to work together might include:

⇨ Discuss and share best practices for networking

⇨ Create a listserv or a social media page to share events and programs and ideas

⇨ Critique each other's pitch

⇨ Attend events and programs together

⇨ Join a charity or sit on a charity board (a great way to meet people and learn about operations)

⇨ Make referrals

⇨ Share experiences

PART 3

Continue to build your network strategically by working with your coach and your new peer group to engage with the people you would like to add to your network. Use the network matrix you built earlier as a guide.

Chapter 7

"*Do not judge me by my success; judge me by how many times I fell down and got back up again.*

—Nelson Mandela

MOTIVATION

There are many stories of the failures of well-known entrepreneurs. For example, *Traf-o-Data,* Bill Gates's failed startup was instrumental in teaching him important lessons needed to start Microsoft. One thousand restaurants reportedly rejected Colonel Sanders's fried chicken recipe before he started his own line of restaurants. Sir James Dyson created more than 5,000 prototype flops on the way to developing his extremely successful Dyson vacuum.

From Gates, Sanders, and Dyson to the local shop owner, virtually all entrepreneurs have failed at one time or another along the pathway to success. Every entrepreneurial experience is an experiment. The very practice of entrepreneurs is about making and testing assumptions to reach the desired outcome. Along the way, outcomes will often not match expectations. At the same time, we know that for successful entrepreneurs, ultimate failure is not an option. To persevere, every entrepreneur has to have some measure of resilience.

This is the third phase of the ***See, Do, Repeat*** *practice of entrepreneurship.* The ability to see opportunities and the willingness to act on them gets the entrepreneur to the starting line, but winning the race requires resilience. We aren't born with a "how to" manual for life. There isn't a map that shows us how to navigate all of life's twists and turns and road junctures. The same is true for entrepreneurship. There are many books, like this one, that can tell us about entrepreneurship. Many people will share their stories of entrepreneurship. In the end, it is only in the practice of entrepreneurship – returning daily and executing past failure – that will allow you to reach your entrepreneurial vision.

DEFINITIONS, KEY CRITERIA AND CONCEPTS

DEFINITIONS

⇨ **Resilience** – the capacity to recover quickly from difficulties; toughness

⇨ **Entrepreneurial resilience** – the ability to change and adapt, as needed, to ensure the wellbeing of the entrepreneur and the organization

▸ **Personal resilience** – the entrepreneur's ability to recover from challenges and to maintain personal health and wellbeing that will allow good decision-making

▸ **Business resilience** – the ability of the organization to rebound after stress and maintain or recover financial health

KEY CRITERIA AND CONCEPTS

⇨ Entrepreneurial resilience is one of the key drivers of success

⇨ Ensuring personal resilience

- ► Mental agility – switching from reacting to responding

- ► Reframing – seeking to see the problem from a different perspective

- ► Backup plans – optional plans in case the original one doesn't work

- ► Don't accept failure as an option –failure can be a step forward instead of the end

- ► Refocus – learning to put our energy where we can have some control

⇨ Ensuring organizational resilience

- ► Diversity – having multiple product lines, revenue sources, multiple customer groups, backup plans and multiple perspectives

- ► Efficiency – bootstrapping, operating with a low-cost structure where possible

- ► Adaptability – ability to respond quickly and effectively to change

- ► Cohesion – having unity of vision, focus and mission

EXERCISES AND APPLICATION FOR YOUR PRACTICE

Before you begin the exercises in the chapter, complete the following:

WHAT ARE MY LEARNING GOAL(S)

MY MOTIVATION

WHO WILL HELP HOLD ME ACCOUNTABLE?

WHAT ARE MY CURRENT STRENGTHS?

HOW DO I KNOW WHETHER I HAVE REACHED MY GOAL(S)?

ARE THERE OTHER PEOPLE I CAN LEARN WITH OR FROM?

WHAT ARE MY CURRENT CONSTRAINTS?

KNOWLEDGE ASSIGNMENT

PERSONAL COMMITMENT REQUIRED:
30 MINUTES

Like life, the practice of entrepreneurship includes the good days and bad days. It includes highs and lows. There are days when every customer says yes, and days when you aren't sure you will make payroll. There may be times when yet another prospective investor rejects you, or you face another failed product test. The ability to respond effectively, in all circumstances, is the differentiating factor in the successful practice of entrepreneurship. A good place to start is with self-awareness.

Resilience Inventory: Complete the following table. List at least three to five times when you recovered from a loss or disappointment in your life. The three stages of resilience include being prepared, adapting and recovering. For each situation listed, make notes on how you prepared, how you adapted and recovered. Make notes on what you have learned.

| SITUATION | WAS I PREPARED? | HOW WELL DID I ADAPT? | HOW DID I RECOVER? | WHAT HAVE I LEARNED? |

APPLICATION ASSIGNMENT

Personal Resilience: Reflect on the resilience inventory you completed in the previous exercise. Now think about what you have learned in this chapter. Return to chapter 7 of *See, Do, Repeat: The Practice of Entrepreneurship* to get more insight. This week, take 25 to 45 minutes to consider your own personal level of resilience and develop a plan to build your own personal resilience. Are there areas of your personal health you need to address? When you consider your own experiences with failure or extreme adversity, can you respond effectively? Reflect on what you learned. Can you incorporate those lessons into your life?

Venture resilience: Now consider your concept, venture or current/future business. Are the elements of a resilient venture present in your plan or your organization? What kind of changes might help your business remain healthy and resilient to adversity?

MASTERY ASSIGNMENT

Develop a resilience plan: The three stages of resilience include being prepared, adapting and recovering. After considering what you learned in your resilience inventory and journal reflections, create a plan for building personal and venture resilience. Fill in the table below and ask your coach or a trusted peer to help hold you accountable. Your goals might focus on personal issues like getting more sleep so you can handle stressful circumstances well, or they may focus on adding a new source of revenue in your business to reduce dependence on your current revenue stream. Make sure your goals are SMART (Specific, Measurable, Attainable, Relevant and Time-Bound).

Reflection and accountability: Take time to reflect on how well you're doing with working toward the goals in your resilience plan. Periodically, take five to 10 minutes of your time with your coach or trusted peer group to discuss your progress. As you meet goals and feel more confident in your own ability to respond to challenges, celebrate your success and continue to build on this plan with new goals that will help you grow.

My Resilience Plan

OBJECTIVE AND ACTION STEPS	SUCCESS MEASURES	TOOLS AND RESOURCES	MOTIVATION	TIME FRAME AND MILESTONES

Chapter 8

> **"** *Success is the ability to go from one failure to another without loss of enthusiasm.*
>
> —Winston Churchill

MOTIVATION

Entrepreneurs learn that it is better to fail early and fail fast. Getting to success sooner rather than later is about figuring out what won't work. This is the essence of the repeat phase of the **See, Do, Repeat** model. The ability to persist and reach any kind of success in entrepreneurship lies in our willingness to execute past failure.

For most of us, just reading or saying this word can lead to a queasy feeling in our stomachs. Thinking about failing often feels a bit like thinking about death. Fear is a survival instinct that is one of the most basic of human emotions. Fear helps protect us. Yet, we often experience fear under conditions that are not truly dangerous to us.

We imagine and project outcomes that never occur. We ruminate but to reach success, we have to get past this. Overcoming this kind of fear is about reframing how we think about it. It may even require changing how we define it. Overcoming a fear of failure requires awareness and acceptance.

DEFINITIONS, KEY CRITERIA AND CONCEPTS

DEFINITIONS

⇨ **Failure (general)** – an act or instance proving unsuccessful

⇨ **Failure (personal)** – feeling bad because of an unsuccessful outcome; feelings of shame, guilt, regret, humiliation from mistaken choices or decisions

REFRAMING FAILURE

⇨ **Failure doesn't have to be personal;** it relates to an action or decision a person makes, but it is not the entire essence of the person.

⇨ **Failure is temporary;** it is an outcome from an action or an instance that may impact the future, but it exists now and doesn't dictate the future.

⇨ **Failure is a lesson;** since failure is not necessarily personal nor enduring, a failure can teach you what to do next time you encounter similar conditions.

⇨ **Mistakes and failure are necessary;** because failure is a lesson, we may never reach success if we do not allow for mistakes and failure.

⇨ **Therefore, the greater loss is to avoid acting out of fear!**

COPING WITH OUR FEAR OF FAILURE

⇨ Consider the five components of fear

1   experiencing shame and embarrassment

2   devaluing one's self-estimate

3   losing social influence

4   having an uncertain future

5   upsetting important others

⇨ Learn to recognize your fears. Name them and own them

⇨ Have someone to talk to about your fear

⇨ Have an alternative plan

How

EXERCISES AND APPLICATION FOR YOUR PRACTICE

Before you begin the exercises in the chapter, complete the following:

WHAT ARE MY LEARNING GOAL(S)

MY MOTIVATION	WHO WILL HELP HOLD ME ACCOUNTABLE?	WHAT ARE MY CURRENT STRENGTHS?

HOW DO I KNOW WHETHER I HAVE REACHED MY GOAL(S)?	ARE THERE OTHER PEOPLE I CAN LEARN WITH OR FROM?	WHAT ARE MY CURRENT CONSTRAINTS?

KNOWLEDGE ASSIGNMENT

PERSONAL COMMITMENT REQUIRED:
1 HOUR

EXERCISE 1

10 questions to ask yourself about your fear of failure as an entrepreneur:

> **IN THE PAST, WHAT CAUSED YOU TO BE ANXIOUS?**

> **IN THE SITUATION(S) ABOVE, WHAT SPECIFICALLY LED TO THE ANXIETY? WHICH OF THE FIVE COMPONENTS OF FEAR LISTED ABOVE WAS PRESENT?**

> **WERE YOUR FEARS REALIZED? IN OTHER WORDS, DID THE OUTCOME RESULT IN THE LOSS YOU FEARED?**

HAVE YOU EVER AVOIDED CERTAIN OPPORTUNITIES (NEW JOBS, MEETING NEW PEOPLE, PURSUING AN INTEREST, ETC.) BECAUSE YOU WERE AFRAID YOU WOULD FAIL? IF SO, HOW DO YOU FEEL NOW ABOUT THOSE DECISIONS?

HOW DO YOU FEEL ABOUT CHANGE?

ARE YOU COMFORTABLE WITH AMBIGUITY AND UNCERTAINTY ABOUT THE FUTURE?

ARE YOU AFRAID OF WHAT OTHER PEOPLE THINK OF YOU? IF SO, WHAT SCARES YOU THE MOST?

WHEN YOU THINK ABOUT YOUR OWN ENTREPRENEURIAL DREAMS, WHAT SCARES YOU THE MOST?

ARE YOU AVOIDING IMPORTANT ACTIONS OR DECISIONS RIGHT NOW THAT MIGHT BE GETTING IN THE WAY OF YOUR ENTREPRENEURIAL DREAMS?

ARE THERE STEPS YOU CAN TAKE TO OVERCOME ANY OF THE FEARS YOU NOW HOLD ABOUT PURSUING THE NEXT PHASE OF YOUR ENTREPRENEURIAL PASSION?

EXERCISE 2

Explore how you learn from failure

Think of a time that you failed, that is, when the outcome wasn't what you wanted. Now consider these questions.

WHAT WENT WRONG?

WHAT WOULD YOU DO DIFFERENTLY IF YOU COULD GO BACK IN TIME AND MAKE DIFFERENT CHOICES?

WHAT DID YOU LEARN FROM THIS EXPERIENCE?

APPLICATION ASSIGNMENT

PERSONAL COMMITMENT REQUIRED:
1-2 HOURS CONVERSATION WITH TRUSTED PEERS
OR A MENTOR, TAKING NECESSARY ACTIONS

ADDRESSING FEAR OF FAILURE

Reflection: Review your answers to the questions in both exercises above. Did you find out that you are most concerned about the uncertainty that pursuing a startup will bring? Do you need more structure than an entrepreneurial pursuit will provide? Are you most afraid of how others might judge you if you fail? Or perhaps you can't support yourself or your family with this venture financially? Regardless, having fears with any new endeavor is natural and normal. The question is whether you decide to let those fears stop you. Spend time reflecting and write your thoughts in your journal.

Taking action: Based on your reflections, what can you do now to help you overcome one of the fears you identified. Write out three actions you can take. For example, if you are most afraid of the lack of structure that an entrepreneurial venture provides, how can you create your own structure so that you can become more comfortable with this way of working. If you will be working from home when you start, can you create a schedule and routines that will provide structure?

Can you set up meetings throughout the week that can provide you with input from others? Or, if you are afraid you will fail financially, can you do more research or learn more about business finance so that you're better informed? Or can you have a backup plan that will allow you some freedom to explore your entrepreneurial venture on a part-time basis? Or, if you are concerned about what others will think, can you talk to a trusted friend and get some advice?

Now that you have named your greatest fears about your entrepreneurial venture, pick one and list three actions you will take *this week* to reduce some of the anxiety you're feeling. Acting will immediately bring some control and will reduce your fears. Start today!

ACTION 1

ACTION 2

ACTION 3

MASTERY ASSIGNMENT

In the first two sets of exercises, you have taken the first steps toward understanding, reframing and conquering your fear of failure. Mastery, on the other hand, takes a lifetime. Fortunately, you have taken the first steps toward this goal. As you continue your entrepreneurial journey, having a strategy for coping with fear and failure can be extremely empowering.

The first step is allowing ourselves to acknowledge our fears. Instead of avoiding them or ignoring them until they have grown so significant that we are physically or mentally in pain, it is important to see our fears early and act where we can.

Identify three goals in your entrepreneurial venture that you have not pursued because of fear of failing. Fill out the table below and share this with your mentor and perhaps a trusted peer. During the next 30 days, make notes and keep track of your actions and the outcomes. See what you've learned. Use this model in your own journal regularly to continue to stay motivated. Share this with your coach or mentor for help.

GOALS THAT I AM AFRAID TO PURSUE:

WHY (LIST 1 OR MORE OF THE 5 COMPONENTS OF FEAR):

ACTION I PLAN TO TAKE: **OUTCOME FROM THAT ACTION:**

ACTION I WILL TAKE NOW: **OUTCOME FROM MY SECOND ACTION:**

NEXT STEPS:

GOALS THAT I AM AFRAID TO PURSUE:

WHY (LIST 1 OR MORE OF THE 5 COMPONENTS OF FEAR):

ACTION I PLAN TO TAKE: OUTCOME FROM THAT ACTION:

ACTION I WILL TAKE NOW: OUTCOME FROM MY SECOND ACTION:

NEXT STEPS:

GOALS THAT I AM AFRAID TO PURSUE:

WHY (LIST 1 OR MORE OF THE 5 COMPONENTS OF FEAR):

ACTION I PLAN TO TAKE: **OUTCOME FROM THAT ACTION:**

ACTION I WILL TAKE NOW: **OUTCOME FROM MY SECOND ACTION:**

NEXT STEPS:

Chapter 9

> " *Optimism is a strategy for making a better future. Because unless you believe that the future can be better, you are unlikely to step up and take responsibility for making it so.*

—Noam Chomsky

MOTIVATION

The expectation of positive outcomes at the core of dispositional optimism also facilitates continuous investment in the business and leads to the ability to persevere in difficult times. Optimists tend to find it easier to succeed as an entrepreneur. Why is this the case?

Optimism plays an important role in seeing opportunities. People with a positive view of the future think in a way that actually supports many of the skills necessary for opportunity recognition. They hold a positive view of the future and are more likely to find innovative solutions and care for themselves.

Given their more positive view of the future, it is not surprising that optimists are more likely to be willing to move forward than pessimists and have higher levels of self-confidence in their ability to succeed in reaching their goals. They tend to be less likely immobilized by uncertainty, and they have an almost unlimited belief in their ability to keep growing and stretching. Optimism encourages action.

Optimism also leads to greater persistence and resilience. Optimists have better coping strategies, better adaptations to problems and change, have lower levels of anxiety and depression, and are more likely to demonstrate high levels of resilience in the face of adversity.

DEFINITIONS, KEY CRITERIA AND CONCEPTS

DEFINITIONS

⇨ **Optimism** – hopefulness and confidence that the future will be positive (from Latin *optimum* meaning "best thing")

⇨ **Pessimism** – a lack of hope or confidence in the future (from Latin *pessimus* meaning "worst")

⇨ **Disposition** – a person's inherent quality of mind (from Latin *disponere* meaning "arrangement")

⇨ **Dispositional optimism** – tendency to expect good outcomes

⇨ **Dispositional pessimism** – tendency to expect the worst outcomes

⇨ **Realistic optimism** – ability to find a balance between the negative and positive

UNDERSTANDING OPTIMISM

⇨ Optimism and pessimism are at polar ends of a continuum.

⇨ Dispositional optimism or pessimism refers to how a person "arranges" what they see in the future – either tending toward positive or negative on the continuum.

⇨ Dispositional optimism or pessimism is an enduring tendency but is not a personality factor, and the entrepreneur can therefore modify or change with intention.

⇨ Too much or too little optimism can both be dangerous for an entrepreneur.

⇨ Realistic optimism is based on a positive view of the future that provides courage to move forward with an honest understanding of the situation.

LEARNED OPTIMISM[10]

⇨ The opposite of learned helplessness, *a feeling of being unable to change negative circumstances*

⇨ Accomplished through a process of recognizing and challenging pessimistic thoughts

⇨ Reflecting on your own mental patterns with respect to personalization, pervasiveness and permanence are an effective way to move toward a more optimistic perspective

⇨ One method of approaching the process is to use a reflection method referred to as the ABC technique.[11] This approach includes reflecting on self-talk during a negative outcome to better understand what you are thinking about

A the adversity (A) you are experiencing

B your beliefs (B) about that adversity

C and the consequences (C) you are expecting

How

EXERCISES AND APPLICATION FOR YOUR PRACTICE

Before you begin the exercises in the chapter, complete the following:

> **WHAT ARE MY LEARNING GOAL(S)**

MY MOTIVATION

_____

_____

_____

WHO WILL HELP HOLD ME ACCOUNTABLE?

_____

_____

_____

WHAT ARE MY CURRENT STRENGTHS?

_____

_____

_____

HOW DO I KNOW WHETHER I HAVE REACHED MY GOAL(S)?

_____

_____

_____

ARE THERE OTHER PEOPLE I CAN LEARN WITH OR FROM?

_____

_____

_____

WHAT ARE MY CURRENT CONSTRAINTS?

_____

_____

_____

KNOWLEDGE ASSIGNMENT

PERSONAL COMMITMENT REQUIRED:
30-45 MINUTES

EXERCISE 1

Consider a recent negative outcome or adversity you experienced. Reflect on your self-talk during that experience and answer the questions below.

BRIEFLY DESCRIBE THE ADVERSITY YOU EXPERIENCED:

WHAT WERE YOUR BELIEFS ABOUT THE EXPERIENCE (E.G., TO WHOM OR WHAT DO YOU ASSIGN RESPONSIBILITY FOR THE OUTCOME, WAS IT "BAD, HORRIBLE, AWFUL" OR "INCONVENIENT")?

WHAT FUTURE OUTCOMES OR CONSEQUENCES DO YOU ANTICIPATE FROM THIS ADVERSITY?

EXERCISE 2

In the space below, reflect on what you learned from the previous exercise by answering the following questions.

CAN YOU DETERMINE MORE ABOUT YOUR DISPOSITION TOWARD EITHER OPTIMISM OR PESSIMISM?

IF SO, WHAT DID YOU LEARN?

IF YOU COULDN'T MAKE A DETERMINATION FROM THIS EXPERIENCE, CAN YOU THINK OF OTHER SITUATIONS WHERE YOU HAD A NEGATIVE EXPERIENCE TO FIGURE OUT YOUR TENDENCIES TOWARD OPTIMISM OR PESSIMISM?

Use your journal to continue this reflection if necessary or desired.

APPLICATION ASSIGNMENT

PERSONAL COMMITMENT REQUIRED:
1-2 HOURS CONVERSATION WITH TRUSTED PEERS
OR A MENTOR, TAKING NECESSARY ACTIONS

Finding the right balance of optimism is important. Too little or too much optimism can be dangerous. Realistic optimism is based on a positive view of the future, which provides courage to move forward with an honest understanding of the situation. Answer the questions below to help you move into a state of realistic optimism.

REALISTIC OPTIMISM: PART 1

Think about something you would like to accomplish but haven't pursued yet because you're afraid of a negative outcome. For example, you may need money to start your company but don't think a bank or an investor would be willing to invest in you and your business. Or maybe you want to enter a pitch competition but in the past, every time you try to speak in front of others, you freeze so you don't think you would be very good at pitching.

I AM AFRAID TO

WHY AM I AFRAID TO TRY?

WHAT HAVE MY PAST EXPERIENCES TAUGHT ME
ABOUT MY ABILITY TO ACCOMPLISH THIS?

IS MY FEAR BASED ON SOMETHING INTERNAL OR EXTERNAL (E.G., I DON'T
HAVE THE SKILL, THE TIMING IS NOT GOOD RIGHT NOW)?

IS THERE ANOTHER WAY TO THINK ABOUT THIS OR APPROACH THIS?

ARE THERE ANY STEPS I CAN TAKE RIGHT NOW TO HELP ME ENVISION A MORE POSITIVE OUTCOME?

REALISTIC OPTIMISM: PART 2

Meet with your coach or mentor to talk about your answers to the questions above. Share your desires and concerns and work with them to develop a plan to confidently and courageously take positive action.

MASTERY ASSIGNMENT

Learned realistic optimism would provide the courage to act even when others refuse to, and it will help build the resilience necessary to execute past failures. Mastery of learned realistic optimism is about maintaining a positive outlook based on knowledge and understanding of yourself, your business and the world you exist in. These skills take a lifetime, but you can start today by incorporating the following two practices into your life.

Start today by taking the time regularly to reflect on the business, not just work in the business.

Inspiration practice: Make it a practice to listen to the stories of entrepreneurs. There are many podcasts available that will provide you with hours of inspiring stories to help keep you motivated and optimistic about the possibilities of the practice of entrepreneurship. Subscribe to several and take the time to listen – maybe while you are preparing dinner or exercising or commuting. To get started, you can try out the En Factor podcast[12] to hear stories of how entrepreneurs got their ideas to start their businesses, how they met with challenges and how they overcame them, that is, how they started, stumbled and succeeded.

Reflective journaling practice: Journaling provides many benefits, including improved mental and physical health. Staying realistic about ourselves and grounding ourselves in gratitude, kindness and service improve realistic optimism. **Take 10 minutes** a day and use the following prompts to help you build learned realistic optimism through reflective journaling.

What am I concerned about today?

Is my concern based in reality?

What can I do today to lessen my concern?

What am I grateful for today?

What kindness can I share today?

Journal pages are available starting on page 147.

Chapter 10

> **"** *If you don't choose yourself, someone else will and the result won't be pleasant.*
>
> —James Altucher

ENTREPRENEURSHIP IS A CHOICE

Entrepreneurship is empowering, transformative and democratic. Entrepreneurs choose themselves. They don't wait for anyone else to choose them. Entrepreneurship doesn't require a specific degree or experience, and it doesn't discriminate by age or demography.

The practice of entrepreneurship is available to anyone. It can be on a very small and intimate scale or as a change agent for the world. It can be within an organizational environment or be a venue for creating a new organization. It can apply in a not-for-profit environment, or it can provide extreme wealth. A single entrepreneurial effort can provide one job or thousands of jobs.

The practice of entrepreneurship is transformative to anyone who chooses the pathway, and it is also a pathway to changing the world. Regardless of how it applies, the principles of entrepreneurship remain the same. It is a learning and doing skill-based practice. The goal is not expertise in every aspect; the goal is to keep learning and execute past failure to reach your definition of success.

Entrepreneurship is a profession that allows you to choose yourself; it requires you do so. To become an entrepreneur is a very personal decision that doesn't necessitate waiting on someone else to hire you or pick you. You make up the game, and you figure out the rules to play on your own team.

However, savvy entrepreneurs understand that choosing themselves is not enough. They also have the job of convincing others to choose them – customers, clients, key employees, investors and partners – if they want to succeed. They know that entrepreneurship is also a team sport – skills and abilities that you have been learning in the **See, Do, Repeat** model of the practice of entrepreneurship.

NEXT STEPS IN YOUR PRACTICE

I make it a practice to discuss next steps before I leave each meeting, important conversation, classroom or training session. Similarly, I am also always thinking about the next steps for my reader. When I wrote the book, *See, Do, Repeat: The Practice of Entrepreneurship*, I concluded with the topic of choosing yourself. This guidebook is not different. I want to leave you with some thoughts and exercises that can serve as a bridge to the next phase in the practice of entrepreneurship, as you decide to choose for yourself.

The 3 *M*'s of choosing your entrepreneurial practice

⇨ Understanding your *Motivation*

⇨ *Managing* your time and energy

⇨ *Making* a commitment

CHOOSE YOURSELF — MOTIVATION

Have you deeply considered why you want to be an entrepreneur? As you now know, entrepreneurship is a lifetime practice. As with any life choice, there are opportunity costs. Answer the following questions as you reflect on the practice of entrepreneurship.

What is my motivation? Check all that apply.

What are my priorities with respect to my entrepreneurial motivation? Rank each of the items you checked.

☐ I want to make a lot of money

☐ Pay my bills

☐ Make a difference in the world

☐ Fix a problem

☐ Be my own boss

☐ Have a more flexible work schedule

☐ Be powerful

☐ Be a star, get attention, gain visibility

☐ Have more influence

☐ Have fun

☐ Work with other entrepreneurs

☐ Other _____

☐ I want to make a lot of money

☐ Pay my bills

☐ Make a difference in the world

☐ Fix a problem

☐ Be my own boss

☐ Have a more flexible work schedule

☐ Be powerful

☐ Be a star, get attention, gain visibility

☐ Have more influence

☐ Have fun

☐ Work with other entrepreneurs

☐ Other _____

CHOOSING YOURSELF — MANAGING YOUR TIME AND ENERGY

Deciding to choose yourself will require a significant investment of your personal resources. You don't have an endless supply of time, energy and money. It *is* a big decision. You may or may not make others happy with your choice. Entrepreneurship, in particular, can at times be a very selfish pursuit. How will this practice fit into the life you have now? Will you need to make any changes?

Our lives usually have several categories of responsibility we allocate our time to. Throughout our lives, we may be pet owners, spouses, parents, daughters, sons, grandparents or grandchildren, caregivers, homeowners, employees, organizational members, friends, volunteers and so on. We have responsibilities to others, but we also have a responsibility to our own health and wellbeing.

Consider your life now and how you allocate your time. What are the responsibilities you now have? In the diagram below, put each of your important responsibilities in the five remaining boxes. With the responsibilities you now have, is there room in this diagram for you to add your new entrepreneurial pursuit in one of the five boxes? Did you run out of room? Are there responsibilities you would or could consider eliminating? Can you barter or outsource any of your responsibilities? With limited time and energy, choosing yourself will likely also be about deciding what has to go.

PERSONAL HEALTH, REST,
EXERCISE, AND SELF-CARE

CHOOSING YOURSELF – MAKING A COMMITMENT

Success is about living up to our commitments. This includes the ones we make to ourselves. Choosing yourself will be fun but challenging. This is life. Unless we know where we're going, we will never know what choosing ourselves means. Reflect on what choosing yourself means in the context of your entrepreneurial practice.

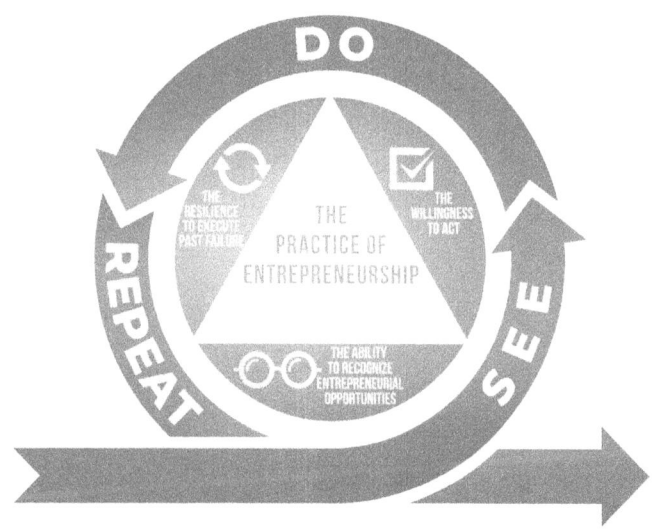

In the next two pages, write down **12 GOALS** for the coming year. A mix of big goals that will stretch you and some that are easier to attain will help you grow and give you a sense of accomplishment. In the end, you are choosing, so just make sure they are meaningful to you. Remember to make sure they are SMART goals (specific, measurable, attainable, realistic and timely). Use these goals to take your next steps in your own personal entrepreneurial practice.

GOAL 1

GOAL 2

GOAL 3

GOAL 4

GOAL 5

GOAL 6

GOAL 7

GOAL 8

GOAL 9

GOAL 10

GOAL 11

GOAL 12

Journal Notes

JOURNAL NOTES

JOURNAL NOTES

JOURNAL NOTES

JOURNAL NOTES

JOURNAL NOTES

Endnotes

1   White, Rebecca J. *See, Do, Repeat: The Practice of Entrepreneurship*. 2021.

2   Casson, M. 1982. The Entrepreneur. Totowa, NJ: Barnes & Noble Books.

3   This process was developed based on James Webb Young's book, A Technique for Producing Ideas and is outlined in much greater detail in the SEE, DO, REPEAT book.

4   This exercise idea comes from Robert McKim and was introduced by Tim Brown (IDEO) at a TED conference in 2008.

5   James Webb Young (from chapter 2)

6   There are many podcasts that share stories of entrepreneurship. You may want to consider The En Factor podcast, which shares inspiring stories of everyday entrepreneurs. You can find it at enfactorpodcast.com or under the name Enfactor on most podcast platforms.

7   Access the See, Do, Repeat reader's discount to take the EMP by visiting emindsetprofile.com/rebecca-white and entering code SDR.

8   Found online at drrebeccawhite.com/see-do-repeat#assessment/

9   According to Guy Kawasaki, one of the Apple employees originally responsible for marketing the Macintosh computer line in 1984 and author of The Art of the Start, the most powerful vision can be reduced to a mantra. A brief, memorable and emotion packed statement the entire team can rally around.

10 A number of psychologists have championed learned optimism; see the work of Martin Seligman, for example. For more see detail on entrepreneurship and learned optimism See, Do, Repeat: The Practice of Entrepreneurship.

11 First introduced by Dr. Albert Ellis and then adapted by Dr. Martin Seligman.

12 This podcast is available at enfactorpodcast.com and on most podcast platforms under the name "enfactor."

EN FACTOR

CONVERSATIONS WITH ENTREPRENEURS

Many of the stories I shared in this book have been inspired by the conversations I have had with guests on my podcast, En Factor™.

Their stories have provided me, and our listeners, with insight, action steps, and motivation towards perusing out entrepreneurial dreams.

To hear more first-hand stories of success, resilience through failure, and how to become a master in your field, please scan the QR code below or visit our website www.enfactorpodcast.com

ENTREPRENEURSHIP IS A WAY OF LIFE

The practice of entrepreneurship is transformative to anyone who chooses to take the journey, and it can also be a pathway to changing the world! The goal of entrepreneurship, is not mastery of every aspect, the goal is to keep learning, to execute past failure, to reach your definition of success.

Dr. White's book captures the true essence of the entrepreneurial journey and unlocks the keys to true success along the way.

—Nick Friendman

The book is perfect for people of all ages of all backgrounds too. Every new venture founder needs to read this book!

—Bert Seither

It is one thing to read about how to accomplish something, but to read stories about real people and how they accomplished their dreams truly inspired me.

—Emily Bagen

Buy your copy today at
See-Do-Repeat.com

Entrepreneurship is as much a business challenge as it is a mental one. Dr. White's new book provides the data for the discipline required to achieve the extraordinary every day.

—Jason Feifer

Available Everywhere Books are Sold: Amazon • Barnes & Noble • Kindle • Nook • Audible

About the Author

Rebecca J. White, Ph.D., is an award-winning educator, entrepreneur, and recognized global thought leader in entrepreneurship. She has developed nationally acclaimed entrepreneurship programs, founded multiple ventures, and contributed significantly to advancing entrepreneurial education.

Her work has earned numerous accolades, including the Karl Vesper Pioneer Award for Lifetime Achievement in Entrepreneurship, the Entrepreneurship Educator of the Year Award from the United States Association for Small Business and Entrepreneurship (USASBE), and recognition in 2019 as one of the Most Influential Board Members in the US by Women Inc. She has also been honored for her excellence in teaching, innovation, and mentorship.

Beyond academia, Dr. White has founded several businesses and advises entrepreneurs and organizations worldwide on innovation and value creation. Today she is Chairwoman of the board at MarineMax, she runs a successful podcast called En Factor: Conversations with Entrepreneurs, and she helps people around the world develop an entrepreneurial mindset and grow their businesses through the See Do Repeat Community found at drrebeccawhite.com.

A resident of Tampa Bay, Dr. White enjoys time with her family, exploring the waters aboard her boat, M/V Resilience, and embracing new adventures.

She can be reached at www.linkedin.com/in/drrebeccawhite and drrebeccawhite.com.